The King Who Couldn't Preach

Kimber J. Lantry

Pacific Press Publishing Association
Mountain View, California
Omaha, Nebraska   Oshawa, Ontario

Dedicated
to Julie

Cover and inside illustrations by Tim Mitoma
Design by Paul B. Ricchiuti

Library of Congress Cataloging in Publication Data

Lantry, Kimber J 1953-
The king who couldn't preach.

(Trailblazers for Jesus series)
SUMMARY: A tenacious Seventh-Day Adventist preacher realizes his place is not in a pulpit, but out in the world, distributing God's literature door-to-door.
1. King, George, 1847-1906—Juvenile literature. 2. Seventh-Day Adventists—United States—Biography—Juvenile literature. 3. Christian literature—Publication and distribution—United States—Juvenile literature. 4. Godsmark, Otho—Juvenile literature. [1. King, George, 1847-1906. 2. Seventh-Day Adventists. 3. Christian literature—Publication and distribution] I. Title. II. Series.

BX6193.K53L36 286.7'3 [B] [92] 80-11333

ISBN 0-8163-0358-4

PREFACE

This book is the second in a series of books for the young child to acquaint him or her with some of the men and women who were trailblazers for Christ in Seventh-day Adventist history. Ellen G. White says that we have nothing to fear for the future except as we forget how God has led us in the past. The purpose of these books is to acquaint our boys and girls with the men and women who have followed Jesus and pioneered the way in God's work, both here in our country and across the sea, and to show the boys and girls of today how God has led in the past.

The books are aimed at children in the beginning reading levels. A selective vocabulary is used. Grades three and four are the grades to which most of the stories are slanted; however, there may be a few books in the set that are geared to fifth-grade reading levels.

This series is the result of the desires expressed by many church-school teachers for extracurricular reading and enrichment in their church-school programs.

It is the hope and prayer of the publishers that these books in the Trailblazer series will assist the children in becoming acquainted with God's leaders and His work, enriching not only the child's knowledge, but his reading and comprehension skills as well.

The Publishers

1

Back when I was little, I didn't like church because I had to sit still for so long. When I got to be eleven, I still didn't like it because I had to wear shoes to church. All summer long I'd go barefoot, but every Sabbath I had to wear shoes, and I hated shoes! The wool socks I had to wear made my feet itch, and the shoes scrunched up my toes.

But every Sabbath morning Mother always reminded me, "Otho, Otho Godsmark, don't you forget to put on your shoes and socks!"

In the wintertime I had to fetch wood for the potbellied stove that heated the church. That meant that every fifteen minutes or so I'd have to get up; put on coat, mittens, and ear muffs; and go outside into the cold for an armload of wood from the woodpile behind the church. Sometimes I'd get splinters in my fingers from the wood even though I wore mittens.

If there were any visitors at church, Dad

would always invite them home for Sabbath dinner. He said it was our "Christian duty." Like as not, they'd end up staying with us that night, which meant that my "Christian duty" was to sleep on the couch in the living room. You see why I didn't like church?

But this particular Sabbath I was almost looking forward to church. That was because Elder James White would be preaching that day. Elder White had a booming voice that made the rafters ring. And he preached pretty good too. Sometimes he'd preach about prophecy. He'd unroll what he called his "prophetic charts." Part of it I couldn't understand—all about prophetic days and weeks and things like that. But on some of the pages he had pictures of great, horrible beasts with lots of heads and horns and other scary things. And he'd always have a story for us children. So you can see why it was I almost looked forward to church that day.

When we drove up to the little church a few miles from our farm in Bedford Township, which is about nine miles north of Battle Creek, Michigan, I could see several horses, with buggies, already tied to the trees. And there outside the church stood Elder White, talking to some of the members. You could tell it was he because he was so tall. He always wore a black stovepipe hat and a long black coat with tails.

I don't remember much about church that day because it was what happened after that got my attention. I do remember that on one of my trips to the woodpile I jerked out a piece of wood and four or five came crashing down, and one hit me on the shin. I hopped around a while on one foot holding my shin until it stopped hurting.

When church was over, Elder White shook hands with the people. Then he came over to my father and put his arm around his shoulder. "Brother Godsmark," he said, "I want to talk to you about something."

I got up as close to Father as I could so I could hear what Elder White had to say.

Whatever it was, it surely seemed to be troubling him. Finally he said, "Brother Godsmark, I've got a man at my house that I just don't know what to do with." He shook his head and then went on. "He's from Canada—somewhere in Ontario, I guess. He's been at my place for at least two weeks. He wants to preach. He says he knows the Lord has called him to preach. Maybe so—" Elder White shrugged his shoulders and spread his hands as if in despair. "But he doesn't look like a preacher to me, and I don't think we can even make a preacher out of him. He's devoted and seems like a good man. But he has no education and can scarcely express himself intelligently." Elder White paused. Then he went on: "I wish you people would take him out on the farm. He can work enough to pay for his board and room. Will you take him, Brother Godsmark? You can see if there is any *preach* in him. His name is King—George King."

I knew even before Father answered what he would say. And sure enough, he agreed.

We got into our buckboard—Mother, Father and I—and followed Elder White's buggy to his house. Father and Elder White went up to the house. I followed them 'cause I wanted to see this man who wanted to preach so badly. He came out onto the porch, and I just stood there and stared at him.

I guess he wasn't very old, but to me—a boy of eleven—he surely didn't look young. He acted very formal and stiff. He couldn't seem to look either my father or Elder White in the eye when he spoke to them. He acted as if he were embarrassed about something.

Come to think of it, he had something to be embarrassed about—his clothes! Now very few people living on farms in those days had much money for store-bought clothes. Mother always did a lot of patching and darning to keep us neat and clean. And I guess all farmer families were like that.

But this Mr. King had on a coat that looked as if it had been through the Civil War and lost. He wore a faded shirt. His pants had a hole in one knee and shiny spots on the seat. His whole outfit looked as if he had slept in a haystack. His shoes looked as if they had never seen polish. They may have been dark brown once, but I could be off a couple of shades.

I couldn't take my eyes off him. But then Mother came up, took me by the arm, and marched me back to the buckboard.

"Othniel Godsmark," she snapped.

Othniel, you see, was my real name; but everybody called me Otho, except Mother—when I was in trouble.

"Don't stare at people like that—especially strangers," she said.

"But he's dressed so funny," I blurted out. "That's what made me stare."

"I don't care how he's dressed. He's one of God's children, and you must be polite and courteous," Mother said.

I wasn't very happy back in the buckboard with Mother. I couldn't hear what the three men were saying. However, after a short while

I saw Father shake hands with Elder White. Then he placed his hand on Mr. King's arm and pointed with his other hand toward the buckboard. Father had a smile on his face, and I knew what had been decided.

I knew I had just lost my bedroom for the rest of the winter. You see, my room was kept warm by a stovepipe that came up through it from the living room downstairs. I'd have to sleep downstairs in the living room.

Father was always doing something for the church. Once—a year ago—Elder White had had another of these talks with Father after church. That talk was something about the publishing work being short of money. The very next morning Father took our two best oxen, Buck and Bright we called them, and gave them to James White to sell. Buck had been my favorite ever since he was just a calf. I used to help hold the milk bucket so he could drink from it. Then Father had to go and sell him. Every time we went into town to the market and stores in Battle Creek, we'd go by the Review and Herald Publishing House and listen to the roar and clatter of the big printing presses. Dad would always say, "Hear that, Otho? That's ol' Buck and Bright still pulling away. They're printing the third angel's message."

I never could figure out what he meant, because I knew they didn't use oxen to run the presses. All I knew was that if Father would give away valuable oxen for the Lord's work, my own bedroom didn't stand a chance.

We headed on home. George King sat up front with Mother and Father. I sat in the back on the floor, shoved and scraped by Mr. King's trunk as we jounced along.

"Well, Brother King," Father said as we rode along, "we're happy to have you spend a couple months with us while you decide what you're going to do."

I could tell that Father was trying to make Mr. King feel welcome.

"I—I've been ah—ah—well, I've felt that—that the Lord ah-ah—wants me to—to—ah—ah—has called me to ah—ah—to preach, Brother Godsmark, sir. That's ah-ah—that's what I—I just have to do."

How could anyone who stammered and stuttered the way this George King did ever hope to become a preacher? I wondered.

"Yes, brother," Father went on, "we want you to do what the Lord has called you to do. But in the meantime, you're welcome to stay with us. You can help out with the chores a little to cover your food and your room."

At the mention of chores, I spoke up.

"That's right, Mr. King. You can help me feed the chickens and churn the butter."

I wanted to make Mr. King feel at home too, and I wouldn't mind it a bit if he helped out with some of my chores. But this was clearly not my day. Mother turned around and gave me one of those looks that made me understand that this was grown-up talk and I was to stay out of it.

Father added, talking as if it was to me, but really aiming at George King, "That's very kind of you, Otho. But Mr. King will be very busy studying his Bible and praying and seeking the Lord's guidance."

"Well," George King began, "well, um, I—ah—ah—thought that, ah—" but before he could make up his mind as to just what he was going to say, Mother cut in.

"Brother King, we want you to consider our home a place of rest and preparation for you so you can be ready to go out into the world and fight against sin and wickedness."

I was going to say that I thought getting up every morning at five o'clock and going out into the cold to feed the chickens would be good preparation for going out into the world to fight against sin, but something in that look Mother had given me made me decide not to say anything.

2

That night I slept downstairs on the big couch in the living room. Mother got out some spare sheets and blankets, and the bed she made on the couch was almost comfortable. I'd have slept good, except for what she said as she was tucking me in."

"Now remember, Otho, we must keep everything neat and tidy; so it will be your job each morning to fold up the blankets and the sheets and put them neatly in the closet in the hall."

Now making my own bed was bad enough, but I knew there would be no way that I could get those blankets folded neatly. Why, they were twice as big as I was. I said so too, with a lot of emphasis.

I don't know whether Mr. King heard me or not, but the next morning a funny thing happened. While I was standing there in my nightclothes looking at those blankets and

sheets and wondering how I'd ever fold them, who should come walking in but Mr. King.

"Otho, do you, ah-ah—think I could help?"

I rubbed my eyes and shifted my weight from one foot to the other. This Mr. King was surely a funny man, offering to help with work. But I wasn't one to miss an opportunity like this. Besides, if it had not been for his coming here, I wouldn't be sleeping on the couch or having to fold the blankets.

"Sure, it's all right with me if you want to help fold them." I figured that would serve him right for getting to sleep in my bedroom.

"Well, Otho, I—I'd be glad to. This is really a two-man job. And, ah, one more thing—it's all right if you call me George."

"A two-man job!" Well, that put it into a different light. I was happy to help out with a man's work. Fetching wood and feeding chickens—that's baby stuff, and I got tired of being treated like a baby, but just ask Otho Godsmark to do a man's work, and you'll really see him go to it.

This Mr. King—I mean George—he really must have folded a lot of blankets, because he showed me how to hold the two corners on my end and bring them together, and then he did the rest of it. Why, in no time at all we had the blankets and the sheets folded and put away.

Of course, you understand, it took two men; and he couldn't have done it half so fast without my help.

As soon as I got dressed, it was time to feed the chickens. George and Father were already at work in the barn feeding the horses and milking the cows. I was struggling along carrying the feed pail when all of a sudden I heard footsteps, and the pail got lighter in my hand. George was walking along beside me helping me carry that pail.

"Otho, we just finished in the barn; so I thought maybe, if it wouldn't be too much trouble, you could show me how to feed the chickens and gather up the eggs."

He didn't stutter at all that time. Now, I was really pretty good at feeding the chickens and gathering up the eggs, and things; so if George wanted to learn how, I figured I could show him.

And I'll have to admit that George caught on pretty fast because in half the time it usually took, I had taught him what to do; and we had all the feed and water out for the animals and headed back to the house for breakfast.

"Otho," George said as we walked along, "I've got a business proposition for you."

"What's a proposition?" I had never heard of that word before.

"Well, it's a deal, an agreement, sort of."

"Oh!" George had a way of making you curious, but I didn't want to seem too interested.

"What I'd like to propose, Otho, is that every day, when I get finished in the barn, I'll help feed the chickens and gather the eggs if you'll do something for me.

Well, I figured I had already done him a favor, teaching him how to feed the chickens; but if he wanted to make a business prepa—, proper—, ah, well, whatever that word was, I guessed that I could at least listen.

"What do I have to do for you?"

"Otho, you see, I think the Lord has called me to be a preacher; and I'm here to learn how to preach. I've got to practice preaching a lot so I can do a good job and so people will want to listen. And I was wondering if, when you have time, you could be my audience and let me practice preaching for you. Do you think that would be fair—I'll help you feed the chickens if you'll help me practice preaching?"

"Does that mean I have to go out every little bit and fetch wood for the stove while you're practicing preaching?" You can see that I'm a pretty sharp businessman; I wasn't about to let him pull a trick on me—a trick that would leave me having to do more work.

But George just laughed. "No, Otho, you won't have to fetch any wood. We're not going to the church. We'll practice here at home, in the living room, or in the barn."

"That's fine with me, George. When do we start—this morning?"

"No, not this morning. I've got a lot of studying to do first, but it will be soon."

That morning, while we were eating breakfast, I got to thinking. This George King, when he was around me, why, he was talkative and interesting; and he'd look me in the eye, instead of staring at the ground—not at all the way he did at church on Sabbath. Maybe, I figured, he just gets nervous when he's around a lot of people.

In any case, with him helping me feed the chickens and fold my blankets in the morning—and all I had to do in return was listen to him preach once in a while—maybe having him come and live with us for a couple of months wouldn't be so bad after all.

3

That winter George preached to me a lot. Sometimes we would take all the chairs in the living room, and in the dining room, and arrange them in rows. Then we would put the end table on top of the piano bench for a pulpit, and I'd pretend to be the audience, all by myself, and listen to George preach.

Sometimes, when Mother needed to work in the house, if it wasn't too cold, we'd go out into the barn. I'd sit up in the hayloft, pretending it was the balcony in some great big church and that the stalls where the cows stood were the pews, filled with people. Way down on the other end of the barn, by the door, George would put a block of wood on a wheelbarrow; and that would be his pulpit. It got awfully cold in the barn sometimes. I'd burrow down under the hay to keep warm, with just my nose sticking out. But George never seemed to notice the cold. All he

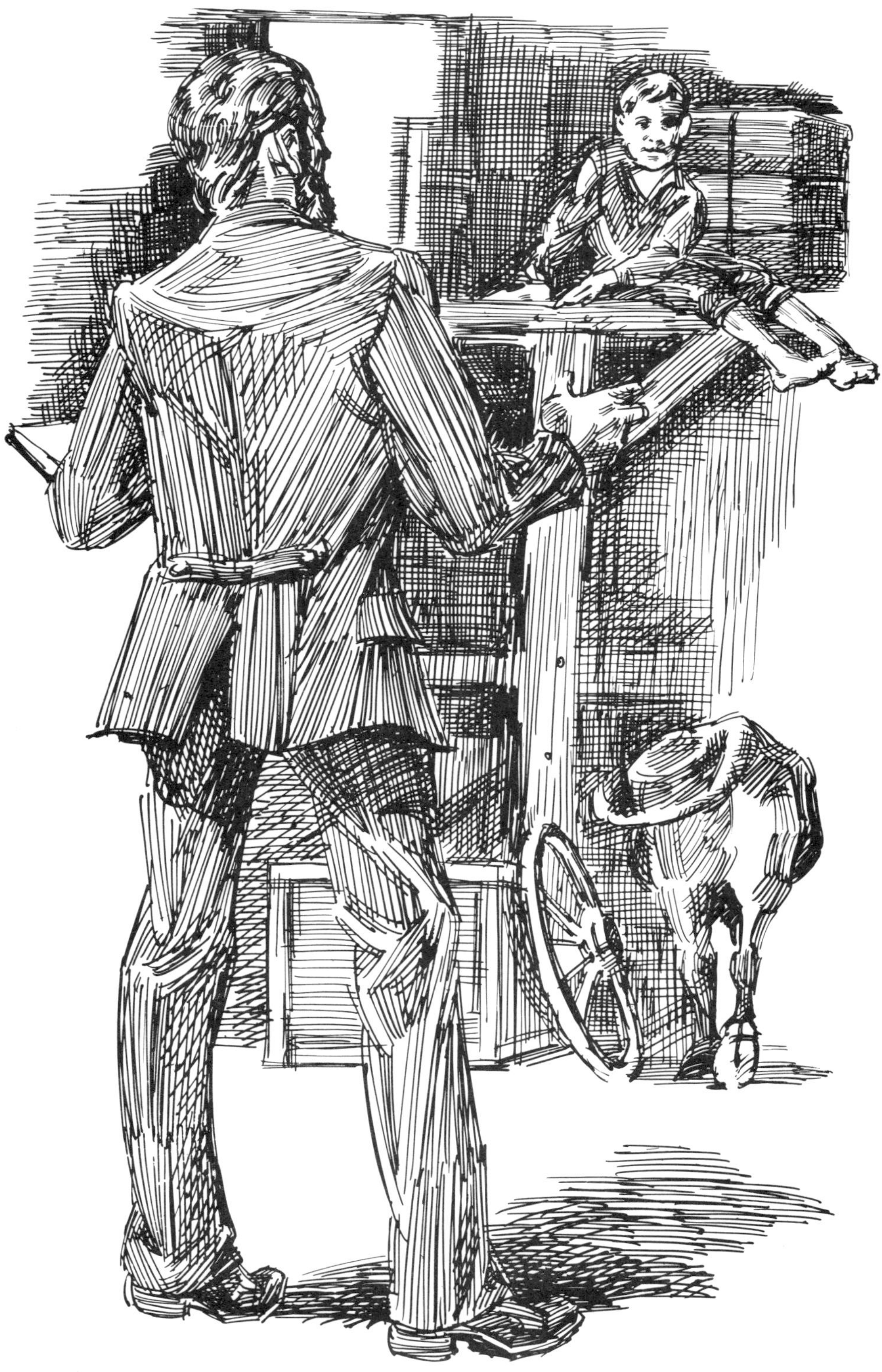

wanted to do was preach.

One day that winter Father went into town to buy some stuff at the market, and he stopped by the Review and Herald Publishing House and bought a roll of those prophetic charts—just like the ones James White used—and two new books that had just been written by Uriah Smith, *Thoughts on Daniel* and *Thoughts on the Revelation.* Those books explained what all the prophecies and the charts meant. When Father got home and gave them to George, George got all choked up and couldn't say anything for a while. He was sort of like I was last Christmas when I got the new wooden train carriage and stayed up late playing with it. That night the candle burned in George's room for a very long time while he read the books, and I went to sleep hearing the rustling of the sheets of the prophetic charts as he turned the pages.

It got so that the whole family was helping George prepare for the ministry. Mother would sit down and go through the Bible and the prophecies with George and make suggestions on the best way to present the charts and the Bible texts to the people. Dad would ask every night how George was coming along. But I was the only one who got to hear George practice preaching. I guess I was special, since I made that business deal, I mean, ah, proposition, with George. Every morning he would help me fold the blankets and feed the chickens. Once or twice Mother offered to help fold the blankets, but I wouldn't let her because it's a two-man job; and if George kept his part of the deal and wouldn't let anybody but me hear him preach, I figured it wouldn't be fair if I let anybody help fold the blankets.

With all of this preaching goin on, I was getting so I knew the prophecies better than anyone else in my Sabbath School class. I could tell you how many heads each beast had and what kind of metal each part of the image was made of, from the head of gold to the feet of iron and clay; and I even knew the name of the country each stood for. And George—why, he preached so good that sometimes, if he had had a black coat and a stovepipe hat, it would have seemed that James White himself was there. I didn't go to sleep very often when George preached either, though it can get mighty warm and cozy when you are snuggled down in the hay in the hayloft.

That's about all we did that winter—the chores and the preaching. Oh, yes, and one thing I almost forgot. George prayed a lot. If he wasn't studying his Bible—you could depend on it—he'd be up in his room with the door closed and on his knees, praying. Once or twice I pressed my ear to the door and listened. It was always the same—something about if it was God's will, that he would become a preacher and lead souls to Christ. I knew that George would do it too; and when he became a great preacher like James White, I would tell everyone how I helped by letting him do the chores and being his audience.

One day toward spring Father and George got to talking at the supper table.

"George," Father said, "it's warming up now, and summer is not far off."

George just sort of mumbled, "I know," and looked down at his plate. He seemed nervous all of a sudden. I couldn't figure out why.

"Summer's the time for holding meetings and for preaching; and I was wondering, how's it coming? Do you still feel the call to preach? Are you ready?"

All of a sudden it seemed George wasn't the same George that I knew. He was stuttering again, just as he did the first day he met us.

"Well, ah-ah, I don't know, er-ah if I am."

"When I was in town last week," Father went on, "I ran into James White, and he asked me about you. How do you feel about it? Do you feel you are ready to take a tent and go out and hold meetings this summer?"

Everybody around the table had stopped eating and was looking at George. George looked down at his food.

Father continued: "I told James White how hard you are studying, and all the practicing you've been doing; and he suggested that we arrange a special service and give you a chance to preach to us. What do you think, George?"

"Well, er—ah, I guess that's, ah-ah, that's what we had better do."

I could see that something was really wrong; so I figured I had better cheer George up.

"George, we'll work extra hard to get the chores done so I can spend more time helping you preach."

George looked up and gave me a kind of a weak smile.

"Yes, Otho, we'll do that."

"Great," Dad said. "I've invited all the neighbors around for a couple of miles for Sabbath dinner," Dad said. "Afterward you can preach to us on the prophecies or whatever the Lord tells you to speak on."

"Will Aunt Huldah be coming?" Mother asked.

"Yes, she's invited," Dad answered.

At the mention of Aunt Huldah's name I got excited. You see, Aunt Huldah was a great big lady. I won't say she's fat, because I got a spanking for saying that once; but she always brings a plate full of cookies for me, and she laughs a lot, and she can tell interesting stories too. I always look forward to having Aunt Huldah come to visit.

I was going to ask Mother what kind of cookies she was bringing this time, when George interrupted.

"I think that, ah-ah, I'd, well, I'm really not too hungry, and I'd rather go to my room for a while, if you, ah, could, ah—be so kind as to—to excuse me."

Father nodded in an understanding way; and I forgot all about the cookies, wondering what it was that was bothering George and how I could help cheer him up.

4

That day when George was going to preach to everyone, I woke up early, very excited. Today was the day when George and I would show everyone what we had accomplished out in the barn, practicing preaching all winter long. For some reason George didn't come downstairs and help me fold my blankets. I struggled awhile, trying to get the corners together; but, as George said, it was a two-man job; so I finally gave up and stuffed them into the hall closet and hoped Mother wouldn't open the door and find out.

George finally came down for breakfast, after all the rest of us had started eating; but he didn't seem like himself and ate only a little. Even though it was spring, the day was chilly; but George insisted on going out in the barn to practice preaching one more time. I volunteered to go help him, but Mother shook her head.

"No, Otho, not this time. I think George needs to be alone."

Just before lunchtime, Aunt Huldah and several other families drove up; and it was exciting to have my nearest neighbor, Johnny, visit us and to tell him how George was going to be such a great preacher and how I had helped.

Aunt Huldah brought a plate of sugar cookies, which were my very favorite, except for peanut-butter ones, and Mother let me have two cookies, since it was a special day. George didn't come back from the barn. He even skipped lunch; so I saved one of my cookies in my pocket for him, except when I sat down the cookie got all crumbled. So I ate the little pieces. I figured George would understand.

After lunch the men moved the dining-room table out of the way and arranged the chairs in rows, like at church. I showed them how George set up the end table on the piano bench to make a pulpit, and Father got George's prophetic charts and hung them on a nail on the wall in front of everybody. I had seen them so often that I knew all the pictures, but I guess everybody else hadn't seen them as much.

George had come in from the barn and was

waiting up in his bedroom. We all sat down, and Father told everyone how the Lord had called George and how he had come to live with us, to prepare for the work; and now we were to see if he could be a preacher. I was hoping Father would say something about how I had helped, but I guess he forgot. We all bowed our heads, and Father offered a prayer asking the Lord's blessing on George and that His will be done. Then we all said Amen. I said so too because I knew that George was going to give a good sermon just like he gave in the barn.

Then George came downstairs. He had with him his Bible and his two books on Daniel and Revelation. He set them all down on the pulpit, but one of them was too close to the edge, and it fell off. Five or six pages of notes fell to the floor too. Fortunately I was sitting on the front row, and I helped George gather them up, but I didn't look to see how the pages were numbered.

George started to speak, and I guess it was going to be on the beasts in Daniel 7, but he got mixed up between the prophecies and was talking about the goat with the one horn, and the ram, when he should have been talking about the four-headed leopard. I guess it was my fault. When he dropped his notes, I didn't get them back in the right order.

I don't remember much about what happened after that, but things didn't get any better. George just kept looking down at his Bible and mumbling and talking as if he wasn't sure what to say next. I knew he could do better, because in the barn he always looked up and didn't stutter at all. He went to turn the page of his prophetic chart, and it didn't fold over quite right; so he tried a little harder, and it got a big tear right down the middle. Johnny, the neighbor boy, who was sitting next to me on the front row, started to snicker; so I kicked him a good one right in the shin. He should have known better than to laugh when George was doing the best he could. But Johnny didn't know better; instead, he turned and punched me in the arm. I was going to punch him back, but Mother came and marched me back to sit with her.

I rubbed my arm, which hurt quite a bit; so I don't remember exactly what George said, except at the end. He said that he hoped everyone would excuse him, but that that pretty well covered the beasts in Daniel chapter 7 and that he begged their pardon if he wasn't too clear on everything, and he hoped that they had all understood, and that was all he had to say. With that, he picked up his

Bible and his books on prophecy and went back up to his room. Nobody said anything. You could hear each footstep on the stairs. He went into his room and closed the door.

Even then nobody said anything. Dad scratched his head. Mother looked at her hands. Johnny snickered again. I rubbed my sore arm. Aunt Huldah stared at the rip in the prophetic chart.

Finally, Father cleared his throat a couple of times, stood up, and asked if anyone had been impressed if the Lord had called Brother King to preach, or what?

I was impressed that George hadn't had a fair chance, because it wasn't his fault that his book fell off the pulpit or that his chart ripped or that Johnny snickered; but just before I spoke up, Mother did.

"It's clear to me that Brother King has not been called to preach the same way others preach," Mother said. "Brother King can never go up to the pulpit and hold the attention of a crowd. But I believe completely the same thing Brother King believes—that he has been called to work for the Lord. I think he might succeed as a preacher of a different type—what we might call a fireside preacher. He could go to the homes of people and preach to them around their firesides, give them tracts and other good literature, and talk about the truth to the people."

You know, the more I thought about it, sitting there in the back row swinging my legs back and forth, the more I could see that Mother was right. George did real good whenever he practiced preaching to me in the barn, but he got nervous when he had to get up in front of a bunch of people. While I was thinking, Father spoke up again:

"If Brother King will agree to follow such a plan, the Godsmark family will stand behind him because we believe in his calling. We'll buy all the tracts that he'll need and furnish whatever money necessary for his expenses that he can't earn himself. In fact, Mother, if you'd agree, I'd say that as long as Brother King devotes his life to such a work, he can have a home with us and will never lack food, clothes, money for expenses, and tracts."

"I certainly agree," Mother said, almost before Dad stopped talking.

I agreed too. In fact, I thought it was just great that George could stay with us; so I spoke up: "He can even keep my bedroom."

Aunt Huldah, Father, and some of the others smiled. I could see they were glad that I was willing to help.

We called George back down. At first, as he

came back into the room, he was really nervous, but as Father talked, outlining what we proposed to do, I could see George smiling and nodding his head in agreement. When Father had finished, George spoke up.

"Brothers and sisters," he said, "I feel that the Lord has spoken through you today—this is the call of God. All this time I had thought there was only one way I could preach—in the pulpit. I knew I had been called to preach, but I was so afraid that I couldn't succeed in the pulpit. Now I see that God calls us to preach in different ways, and I know this is how He would have me preach."

After that we all bowed in prayer and thanked the Lord for His leading, and then everyone began to talk at once about how George would go out and preach. Everyone that is, except Aunt Huldah. She went and got her plate of cookies and a pitcher of milk and set them on the table, and pretty soon everyone was munching on cookies—especially George and me. I didn't keep an exact count, but I think this was one time when he ate more cookies than I did.

5

The very next Monday morning George left home to begin his fireside preaching. Mother spent all day Sunday patching and mending George's clothes so he looked presentable. Father climbed up in the attic and found an old handbag that George could carry his tracts and his Bible in. We went through all the drawers and sorted out the tracts and literature, and George put all he could get into the handbag. Mother made George a big lunch—enough food to last him a week if he could carry it. I emptied my savings bank, and Mother helped me count the money. I had 34 cents saved up, and I wanted to use it to help George with his expenses. Father added some more money; so George had two dollars to take with him that week—more money than I had ever had. Everyone agreed that George would return next Friday night and go to church with us the next Sabbath.

Monday morning bright and early I got up. George came down as usual to help me fold the blankets. By this time I had gotten pretty good at folding blankets; so George would hold his two ends while I did all the rest.

"George," I said as we were putting the blankets away, "does this mean that I get my bedroom back?"

"Well, you'll have to ask your mother, Otho, but it looks like it."

"And you won't help me fold the blankets or feed the chickens anymore?"

"Well, maybe next Sabbath, when I come back—"

"And we won't go to the barn and practice preaching anymore?" I wanted to know.

"No, Otho, I'm through practicing. Now I must go out and be a fireside preacher and give out tracts and tell people about the prophecies."

I felt a lump in my throat; but I didn't cry, because that's baby stuff.

After breakfast the family said good-bye to George and waved as we left the house together. I walked with George as far as the main road to give him a hand with his bag of literature. He carried the lunch, which was so big that I pointed out he might as well eat it now. That would be easier than carrying it.

He stopped and took out the cookies that Mother had stuffed inside the lunch bag and gave them to me, "to lighten his load," he said.

Then he was off, walking up the road; and in no time at all he went over the rise and out of sight. I waved and waved until I couldn't see him anymore. Then I remembered that in all the excitement I had forgotten to feed the chickens, and then it hit me that I would have to do it all by myself again. I sat down under a tree and decided to try one of the cookies, but my mouth was all dry, and the cookie got all lumped up in my throat, and then my eyes weren't dry; and, well, I knew I was really going to miss George.

That whole week dragged by slowly. Sleeping in my own bedroom was nice, but feeding the chickens by myself was hard work. Besides, time just seemed to drag, with no one to practice preaching with. George had left his prophetic charts with us, since they were too large to carry. I would get them down and turn the pages carefully, trying to remember what George had said about each beast and what it stood for.

Friday afternoon I helped Mother clean the house and took my bath early so when George got home, he wouldn't have to wait to get cleaned up. But George must have been late.

Mother set the table with an extra plate again, for George, and waited supper until I couldn't wait any longer; but George still didn't come.

We sat around the fireplace in the living room, with Father reading out of the Bible. He read the story of Samuel all through, and George hadn't come yet; so he read the story or Saul, the first king, and still George hadn't come. Then he started on the story of David, but I don't remember much about that because I couldn't keep my eyes open. I don't remember going up to bed. The next thing I remember, it was morning. As soon as I realized it was morning, I knew George must have come; so I jumped out of bed yelling, "George, George."

He didn't answer; so I figured he must be sleeping on the couch downstairs, where I usually slept. I went to the living room, but he wasn't there. Just then Mother came downstairs.

"Otho," she said, "George didn't come in last night."

"Is something wrong, Mother?" I could feel a lump coming into my throat.

"I don't think so. Don't worry. George probably had so far to walk that he stayed with someone else along the way. We'll probably see him at church."

I didn't think so, but I didn't want Mother to worry; so I was brave and said that I figured that is what must have happened.

But on the way to church, in the buckboard, I had a real battle with that lump in my throat again. I strained my eyes as we came over the last rise in the road. There was the church, and several folk outside. Then I let out a yell.

There, standing in front of the church, was a man in an overcoat that I would know anywhere. George was back! When he saw our wagon and heard me yell, he waved his hand. I jumped off the buckboard and ran ahead.

I dashed up and threw my arms around him. Everybody else wanted to shake his hand. The people slapped him on the back, and it seemed everyone was talking at once. I don't know what the leaders had planned for Sabbath School that morning, but whatever it was, they forgot about it—because everyone wanted to hear what had happened to George that week. I sat right up in front, as close to George as I could get. Aunt Huldah was there with a fresh batch of cookies, I hoped! Johnny came up and sat in the front row beside me.

"Brothers and sisters," George began, "the Lord has blessed me this week and opened doors, and I can see that there is a great work to be done in this field. Last Monday I started out with a carpetbag full of literature and $2.00 in my pocket—given to me by the Godsmarks, including little Otho there." George pointed directly at me.

Of course, I turned around and smiled so that everyone could see just who had had a part in helping George.

George started at the beginning and told us exactly what had happened each day. I can't remember just everything he said, but it was something like this:

"When I left last Monday morning, Otho, here, walked me out to the road and saw me off. When I walked over the hill and down the road, I was feeling a little lonely; but mostly, I felt excited because I just knew that this was what the Lord wanted me to do and that any minute now I'd come around the corner and find a farmer waiting to hear about the prophecy and become a believer.

"I walked and walked and walked. Folks, I don't really know what road I took. I was just doing the walking, and I knew the Lord was doing the directing. But nothing happened. There weren't any farmers out in the fields. I suppose I had thought I'd find farmers in the field, stopping at the end of a row and waving to come over to preach about the prophecies." He stopped talking, rubbed his hands together, and then went on. "It was too cold, and they all must have been in their barns or gone to town or something. In fact, it didn't seem like there were many farms—mostly just woods.

"After a while I figured that maybe what was going to happen to me would be like what happened to Philip, in the Bible, when the Ethiopian man came along in his chariot, picked Philip up, and wanted to know about the Bible. But no chariots came along."

I laughed out loud because I figured George was trying to be funny, but no one else laughed. I guess they just didn't understand George the way I did.

George went on. "All that morning, nobody came down the road—no farm wagons, no buggies, no one on horseback. Finally, I decided that maybe the best thing to do would be to stop and have lunch and think this over. I was supposed to be a fireside preacher, but how was I going to preach until I got to somebody's fireside."

I laughed again, and still nobody else did. I knew everything was going to come out all right, and George was just trying to make things interesting, but everybody else in our little church seemed to be all worried about how George was going to get to somebody's fireside to start his preaching.

"Well," George said, "that stopping for lunch helped a lot. Mrs. Godsmark had fixed some mighty good food, and she had wrapped it so well that it was still warm; and as I ate, I began to feel a little better. Maybe the Lord wasn't going to send someone in a buggy to pick me up and give me a ride, and maybe the farmers weren't out there waiting to hear about prophecy. Maybe I'd have to go find them myself. I determined that the next house I came to, if the Lord told me to go and knock on the door, that's what I'd do.

"Well, it wasn't but about half a mile farther on that I came over this hill, and there, surrounded by fields and patches of woods, was this barn and this pretty little house, with smoke coming out of the chimney. I guessed that this would be the house the Lord would tell me to go visit, for sure.

"As I got up close, I kept waiting for the Lord to tell me to go ahead, but nothing happened. Last week at the Godsmarks' house I knew for sure that the Lord was telling me to become a fireside preacher. I could just feel it, in here, you know? It's the feeling you get, right down here." George pointed to his heart.

I could see he was having trouble trying to get the idea across. A few people were nodding their heads. I guess they understood. I didn't know just what this feeling was, but I wanted George to feel good; so I nodded my head too.

"Well," George went on, "I didn't feel like the Lord was telling me to go to that house; so I turned around and started back toward the main road. But I didn't feel that was the right thing to do either. I just didn't know what the Lord wanted me to do. Before I could make up my mind, I heard a door slam; and I knew somebody was coming out of that house and he would see me any moment. So that decided it. I got my courage up as best I could and headed back toward the farmhouse.

"A man came out of the house—a really big man, with bib overalls and leather suspenders. He didn't see me. He went into the barn. I figured that would be the best place to catch him—out in the barn—so I went that way.

"The door was off around the side; and just as I came around the corner, he came driving out in a wagon pulled by a team of horses. He appeared so suddenly he scared me, and I dropped my carpetbag full of tracts and let out a little surprised yell. One of the horses must have been skittish, because it started to buck; and the farmer had to jerk the reins hard, yelling, 'Whoa, boy, steady there!' He finally got the horses calmed down. I picked up my carpetbag, adjusted my coat, cleared my throat, and was just going to say something when the farmer turned to me and yelled.

" 'Who do you think you are anyway—sneaking around here, trespassing on other people's property, and frightening the horses?'

"Every other word he said, it seemed, was a curse word, or an oath. His face was all red, and I suddenly noticed that in a holder beside the seat, he had this great big horsewhip all curled up.

" 'Well, sir,' I replied, 'I'm a fireside preacher. And I'm here to tell you about the Bible, and prophecies, and—'

" 'Preacher,' he yelled, 'you don't look like a preacher. You look like a tramp, or one of those hobos who ride around on freight trains. Likely story, a preacher,' he muttered, and got down off the wagon and flipped the reins over a hitching post.

"As he hopped down off the wagon, I realized what a big man he was. Why, he must have weighed two hundred pounds. The other thing that hit me was, for such a big man he sure jumped off that wagon fast. I caught sight of that horsewhip again, and all I could think of was how much I wished I was back in those woods, because I just knew that the Lord hadn't led me to this house."

George paused. I was getting worried now, and I could see that Johnny, sitting next to me, was worried too, because he was chewing on his fingernails. I stopped swinging my legs back and forth and gripped the edge of the pew real hard with both hands till my knuckles turned white. It just wouldn't be fair, if some mean old farmer who said all kinds of curse words beat George up or whipped him with the horsewhip. After all, it wasn't George's fault that he scared the horses, just as it hadn't been George's fault last week when the prophetic charts got all ripped.

George interrupted my thoughts, continuing with his story.

"Well, this farmer, he says, 'Let's see what you've got in that carpetbag.' He used a lot more cusswords. So I handed over the carpetbag.

" 'It's tracts, sir, and papers—religious stuff. You can, ah, have some, if you'd like.' I didn't know what else to say. Maybe if he took some, he wouldn't be so mad about my scaring his horses. He reached in, pulled out a handful, and dropped the carpetbag. It landed in a mud puddle.

"He stared at the tracts a long time, turning the pages slowly. I wondered if he was interested in learning more about the truth, he was staring at them so hard. I knew they didn't have any pictures on them, just Bible texts and things like that; and I wondered which one he was reading. I edged up closer for a little look over his shoulder.

"What I saw almost made me laugh out loud. I had to clap my hand over my mouth. That big farmer was holding the tracts upside down, staring at them intently. The poor man couldn't read."

What George said made me laugh out loud. This time, so did everybody else. If that farmer hadn't been so mean to George, yelling and cursing at him like that, why, you could almost feel sorry for him. Even I could read a little. As the laughter died down, George went on. "All of a sudden, the farmer noticed me looking over his shoulder, and he got kinda nervous and held the tracts so I couldn't see them. I guess he must have been afraid I would figure out that he couldn't read.

" 'Sir,' I said, 'would you like to keep those tracts and study them in the evenings with your wife? Could I come back and study with you later?' Maybe, I figured, the Lord had wanted me to come here all along. The man paused, lost in thought, for a long moment.

" 'Naw,' he said, picking up the carpetbag and thrusting the tracts back into it, and then handing it back to me. 'I don't got no use for religion, and reading papers, and things. Times are mighty hard, trying to raise a decent crop, feed the stock, and keep the woods cleared off; and I can't be spendin' any time readin' the Bible.'

" 'But your wife, sir, maybe she would read these—they're free. You can have them.' I held the carpetbag out to him, still open.

" 'Yea,' he said, 'the wife, she'd like them all right. She'd really appreciate readin' about God, and the Bible, and things.'

" 'Well, then, take them, sir, for her, from me, please.' I almost pleaded.

" 'Naw, it's too late,' he said. After a long pause he grasped my arm and pointed out toward a grove of trees. 'Ya see that bare spot, on the ground, where there ain't no grass?'

" 'Yes.'

" 'The wife—she's there. She died—consumption. It's too late now.'

"He turned and spent a very long time, it seemed, fumbling with the horses' harness. I stuffed the tracts back into the carpetbag, closed it, and busied myself brushing mud off the bottom.

"Finally the big farmer turned around and said, 'Now go. Be off with you, and don't scare anymore horses. Down the road, a mile and a quarter, or thereabouts, there's a big white farmhouse with two chimneys, one on each side. House is on the north side of the road. Family by the name of Henry lives there. Ya stop there, and tell 'em Mac sent ya. Give 'em your religious stuff and tracts and things. They'll feed ya and put ya up for the night, and they'll want to hear all about Bible prophecies and such stuff. Now git, you've been enough trouble for one day.' He tried to sound mean and gruff, but he couldn't. Down inside, I knew, he was crying, because I heard him choke it back, once or twice."

George paused again. I looked around to see how the other church folks were taking it in. Mother was fishing in her handbag for a handkerchief. Aunt Huldah was already blowing her nose, real loud. Dad seemed to have a twitch in one eye. Johnny was still chewing his fingernails. I figured right now would be a real good time to head for the woodpile, because I didn't want anybody to see me cry.

6

As I walked in with an armload of wood, George started talking again. I guess he must have waited for me so that I wouldn't miss anything. That was just like George; he remembered his friends.

"Well," George said, "when I left that big farmer, Mac, and headed down the road, I must have lost track of time. All I could do was think about Mac, and that bare spot of ground out near the grove of trees, where he had had to bury his wife. She had died only a few months before I got there. If only I'd gone a few months sooner, she would have heard about the truth.

"I was so busy thinking that I must have taken the wrong fork in the road. Anyway, I got completely confused as to where I was or where that house was with two chimneys, the one where the Henrys lived. I kept walking and walking. The sun was going down, and it

4—K.C.P.

was getting cold. Finally, just after the sun went down but while there was still enough light to see my way, I came out of the woods into a cleared area; and off in the distance I could make out a building. I didn't think it could be a farmhouse, because I couldn't see any lights. As I got closer, it turned out to be an old empty shed. Apparently the farmer who worked this land lived some distance away. There was no moon that night, and it was getting really dark; and I knew unless I spotted a light, there was no way I was going to find anything until morning.

"I sat down in the doorway of the shed and waited. No lights appeared. It began to get really cold. I hugged myself with my arms, trying to keep warm, while I decided what to do. Piled up inside the shed was a lot of hay, and it looked more and more inviting all the time. Finally, I walked over, burrowed out a hole in the stack, and crawled in. Just before I got in, I remembered an old trick we had learned up in Ontario when I was a boy. I took off my coat and my shirt, climbed in, and pulled them in after me, and then laid them on top, just like a blanket. People always used to say, You'll be warmer sleeping with your clothes off and using them as blankets than sleeping with your clothes on.

"Well, it was surprising how true that was. In no time, it seemed, I felt warm and drifted off to sleep."

George paused a minute while Dad got up and threw a couple more pieces of wood into the stove. I knew just what George meant about staying warm in a haystack. I remembered how I'd kept warm in the hay out in the barn while George had practiced preaching.

"The next morning," George went on, "I got up at sunrise, brushed the hay off, and put on my shirt and coat. Right in front of the shed, wouldn't you know it, was a well with a hand pump. It had been so dark the night before that I missed it. I washed up as best I could, ate a little breakfast from the food left over, washed it down with that clear, cold water from the well, and headed on my way.

"I was determined to find the house with the two chimneys, where the Henrys lived, and see if that big farmer, Mac, was right—if they were interested in the truth. Since I had gotten so lost the night before, I thought it would be best if I headed back in the direction I had come until I got my bearings.

"About a mile back up the road I found the turn I had missed, and headed down that road. I hadn't been walking more than five minutes when I heard the sound of a horse and buggy. I turned and waved, and the buggy stopped beside me.

" 'Can I give you a ride, stranger?' the man in the buggy asked.

"Well, I was more than happy to catch a ride. It turned out that the man in the buggy was a politician, running in the next election for a seat in the state legislature. He was certainly in the right profession, by the looks of things, because he sure could talk a lot. Why, he hardly let me get a word in, telling me all about the great things he would do for the country if only they would elect him to go to the state legislature up in Lansing. He told me all about the railroads, the schools, the new roads, and the industry that would come; and he promised jobs and money for everyone. Finally, he managed to ask me where I came from. As soon as he found out I was from Canada, and therefore I couldn't vote for him in the next election, he stopped talking long enough so I could tell him about my being a fireside preacher.

"He listened carefully as I told him about the prophecies. I brought out some of my tracts and told him how the Lord was coming, and at that he got very quiet. In no time at all, it seemed, we drove up in front of the drive-way to the house with the two chimneys, and I got out. I offered him a tract, and he held it in his hands, thinking.

"Finally he said, 'Look here, Mr. King. You're a mighty good man, doing a mighty good work, and you're giving all these tracts away free, and not getting any wages either. Nothin's free, not in this life, Mr. King. If there's one thing I've learned in politics, nothin's for free.'

"I was about to ask him, seeing that nothing is for free, how he could promise all those jobs and schools and better roads for nothing, if only the people would elect him; but I decided that it wouldn't be polite; so I kept my mouth shut and let him talk.

" 'Mr. King,' he went on, 'you ought to be selling these tracts and using the money to print more tracts—better ones, with pictures, and maybe even books. Now, I'm not a religious man. I'm not much for this prophetic stuff, but I'll tell you what I'm going to do. You just mention to folks whenever you get a chance that I'm running for the state legislature in the election this fall on the Democratic ticket.'

"He reached into his pocket, pulled out a dime, handed it over to me, and said, 'All right, now, Mr. King, you go do your thing—this fireside preachin' stuff—and if they can afford it, don't give these here tracts away for free. People will appreciate them more—read 'em better too—if you make 'em pay for 'em. Just remember what I've said, now. Nothin's for free, not in this life.'

"With that, he flipped the reins and was off; and I was standing by the side of the road, holding my carpetbag in one hand and a shiny dime in the other, and thinking about what he had said.

"I turned and walked up the drive to the Henry house. It was just like Mac said—a great big two-story farmhouse, with a stone chimney on each side. The farm looked prosperous too—a big barn, a couple of sheds, and fields spreading off in three directions.

"I walked up to the door and knocked. I really felt good, what with that 10-cent piece in my pocket and this new idea about selling tracts; and I even knew the name of the people that would be opening the door any second now. Best of all, I knew the Lord had sent me to this house.

"I knocked a second time. A moment later the door opened, and there stood a lady holding a baby, with another small child peeking out from behind her skirt.

" 'Hello,' I said, 'I'm George King. Are you Mrs. Henry?'

" 'Well, yes,' she said, kinda surprised that a complete stranger would call her by name.

" 'Mac sent me. Mac—you know, from down the road.' I pointed off in the direction I had come.

" 'Oh, yes.' She smiled. 'Please come in. Ah, what is it that you want?'

" 'Well, ma'am, you see, I'm a preacher, sort of. I call myself a fireside preacher, because I don't preach in churches, ma'am; but I talk to people about the Lord, and the Bible, and prophecies, and things, right in their own homes. Mac said that you might be interested.'

" 'Well—' She paused. 'Yes, yes, we are very interested, my husband, especially. He has had this feeling that he should be understanding more of the Scriptures, but he can't make sense out of what he reads. I'm interested too,' she added, as an afterthought.

" 'Is your husband around, Mrs. Henry?'

" 'Yes, he's out in the barn, tending to the stock. Let me show you.'

"She grabbed a coat, and we headed for the barn. Mr. Henry was just as she had said—keenly interested in Scripture—and he seemed very happy to meet me. But he was very busy just then; so he invited me to sit and talk while he worked. He was pitching hay down from the hayloft, and I figured that I could make myself useful; so I set my carpet-bag down, took my coat off, and grabbed a second pitchfork; and we went to work. Well, you all know that pitching hay is hard work."

George paused, and everybody around the church nodded. I had seen my dad do it a lot of times. I knew just how tiring it could be; so I nodded too.

George went on. "Well, we couldn't talk very fast. Mr. Henry, he'd heave down a forkload of hay and ask me a question, and I'd heave down a forkload, and answer it. So it went for about two hours. I told him about how Mac had sent me and about the tracts that I had and just a little about the prophecies, to get him interested. He started asking me questions about the Scriptures, and I could see that he'd done a lot of reading. He knew a lot more about the Bible than most farmers.

"At noontime Mrs. Henry called us to the house. We talked about the Bible all through lunch and into the afternoon.

"In no time at all, it seemed, the sun was going down, and we had the evening chores to do.

" 'I'm much obliged to you, George. It would have taken me twice as long to do the work today without your help. The time went by twice as fast, talking about something that I'm interested in. You'll stay the night, of course?' Mr. Henry invited.

" 'I'd really appreciate it, if it wouldn't be too much trouble.'

" 'Not at all, man, not at all. We don't get many visitors out here; and besides, that's the least I can do to repay you for all your work this afternoon.'

"After a good evening meal and after the children were put to bed, Mr. and Mrs. Henry and I sat around the fire. They lit a couple of kerosene lamps, and we got out our Bibles and started talking. I explained to them the prophecy of Daniel chapter 2, and that interested them so much that I went right into the prophecies of Daniel chapters 7 and 8, with the horrible beasts. It seemed so much easier for me to discuss those chapters with them asking questions while sitting around the fire that evening than to get up in the pulpit and preach about them. I know that you were right, Mrs. Godsmark, when you felt that the Lord had called me to be a fireside preacher."

I saw Mother smile and nod her head. I suddenly realized that all this time George had been talking without stuttering or hesitating or getting all mixed up, the way he had the week before; yet he hadn't practiced for this or made any notes or anything. It was just the way he used to preach to me out in the barn, except a lot more interesting.

George interrupted my thoughts again as he went on with his story. "I gave the Henrys several tracts on the Sabbath and on the prophecies and the second coming of the Lord. Mr. Henry was so excited he wanted to keep right on discussing all of these things, but the fire had burned down, and his wife reminded him it was time to go to bed.

"The next morning we talked all through breakfast and up until I had to be on my way. I went through my carpetbag another time, found a couple more tracts that he was interested in, and offered them to him.

" 'George,' he said, 'after all you've done for me, let me do just a little something for you.' He turned and went into the back room. When he came out again, he pressed something into my hand—three dimes.

" 'Keep it, George, for your expenses. Use the money to buy more tracts, and do come back. I want to study this a lot more.'

"As I left, Mrs. Henry handed me a sack—'to tide you over,' she said. And by the weight of it, I knew there was enough food inside to last at least two days. The Henrys had given me the names and directions to three other families they felt might be interested in the truth and be willing to study the Scriptures. I had my work all lined up.

"And that's the way it went, all week long. Not everyone was interested. Some houses I visited, the people had no money to pay for the tracts; so I gave them away. But enough people were willing to pay so that I sold a total of 62 cents' worth for the week." George held it up for us to see. "I've got that $2.00 from the Godsmarks, plus this money from selling the tracts, that I will use to buy more.

"This fireside ministry," George continued, "I can see it growing into something more—into what I'd call, ah, a colporteur ministry. One thing that politician taught me—nothing is free. I think people will appreciate our tracts and be more likely to read and study them if they have to pay something for them. Besides, the money I make will help cover the expenses of buying more tracts."

It must have been an hour or two that we sat there, listening to all of George's experiences that week. I know I made four or five trips to the woodpile before George finished and sat down beside me on the front row. I whispered to him, "George, you're a good speaker. You'll be a preacher yet. Did you know that?"

I could see that what I said made George feel good, because he smiled and whispered back, "No, Otho, I'm not called to a pulpit ministry. I think that I am called to a different kind of ministry—the literature ministry. But it's just as important."

I nodded, but I didn't really think so. Going from house to house didn't seem half so important as standing up in front of hundreds of people in a great big tent with prophetic charts filled with horrible beasts. I'd talk to George about it later.

George came home with us that Sabbath afternoon and stayed about half the day on Sunday. It was just like old times, with him sleeping in my bedroom and helping me fold the blankets and feeding the chickens Sunday morning. But he was anxious to get going Sunday and left soon after Mother had made him a big lunch and washed and mended his clothes.

7

I didn't know it then, but that was almost the last I would see of George King for seven years. During those first few months he was in the colporteur work, as it was then called, he would come back to Battle Creek every couple of weeks or so to buy more literature; and if he could get the time, he'd come out and stay for the night or be waiting on the church steps as we drove up on Sabbath morning.

But George felt a call to return to his homeland, Ontario, Canada. "There are too many Adventists around Battle Creek," George told us. "In half of the towns there is either a company meeting or a little church, or they hold a tent meeting in the summer. But in Ontario there are miles and miles of farms and cities where no one has ever heard of Adventists—no churches, no tent meetings, no believers. That's where I need to go."

But George couldn't sell enough tracts in his fireside ministry to make a living in Canada. Every six or eight months he would have to quit his selling of tracts and get a regular job helping with the harvest out in the fields or working in some factory to earn enough money to buy clothes and food. But as soon as he had enough saved up, he'd be back to selling tracts and books again. I used to read his letters in amazement, thinking of the sacrificing he went through. Why, he had no regular home. He was always staying with others, usually in the homes of people who had become Adventists through his work. His clothes were often worn out, and he seemed to spend every spare dollar on buying more books and tracts.

In the meantime I had finished every grade in our little rural school and had gone off to the college that had been started in Battle Creek—the year after George had spent the winter at our house. I guess that period, helping George try to become a preacher, must have had an influence on me, because I decided to study for the ministry. I might have tried to become a fireside preacher like George, but I just didn't see how I could live the way he did. Apparently most other Adventist workers agreed with me, because all those years George King was about the only one selling literature on a regular basis. His vision of hundreds of canvassers selling Adventist books just didn't seem to have much chance of becoming a reality.

In the year 1879 something happened that began to change all that. The Lord sent Mrs. White a message which she published as Testimony number 29. In it she said, "By judicious calculation they [the publishing men] can extend the light in the sale of books and pamphlets. They can send them into thousands of families that now sit in the darkness of error.

"Other publishers have regular systems of introducing into the market books of no vital interest. 'The children of this world are in their generation wiser than the children of light.' Golden opportunities occur almost daily where the silent messengers of truth might be introduced into families and to individuals. . . . Hundreds of men should be engaged in carrying the light all through our cities, villages, and towns. The public mind must be agitated. . . .

"Missionaries are wanted everywhere. In all parts of the field canvassers should be selected, not from the floating element in society, not from among men and women who are good for nothing else and have made a success of nothing, but from among those who have good address, tact, keen foresight, and ability. Such are needed to make a success as colporteurs, canvassers, and agents. . . . The efficient colporteur, as well as the minister, should have a sufficient remuneration for his services if his work is faithfully done.

"If there is one work more important than another, it is that of getting our publications before the public, thus leading them to search the Scriptures."—*Testimonies,* vol. 4, pp. 389, 390.

When I read this testimony from the Lord, one phrase really stuck out—about the colporteur, as well as the minister, having sufficient remuneration for his services. If George had enough money for his work, he wouldn't have to quit every few months and work at another job. And, with a little more money, a lot of others would be willing to sell books. Why, I might even give it a try myself.

I didn't know it then, but Dr. John Harvey Kellogg also was reading Mrs. White's testimony and thinking about how it could be applied. Dr. Kellogg, a brilliant man and a leading physician, had founded Battle Creek Sanitarium. He was a writer too. In fact, his latest book, *The Home Hand Book of Domestic Hygiene and Rational Medicine,* was due to come off the Review and Herald presses that very next year. The book was every bit as big as its title. It contained 1600 pages. Dr. Kellogg was thinking about ways to sell it to as many people as possible. He must have noted in particular Mrs. White's comment that "other publishers have regular systems of introducing into the market books of no vital interest" and done a little research. What he came up with was the idea of selling books by subscription.

A publisher would send salesmen out, going from door to door, with a prospectus, a shorter version of the book. The prospectus would include all the pictures, the most interesting sections, and samples of the binding. The salesmen would take orders, or subscriptions, from people willing to buy the books and would then return a few weeks or months later and deliver the books to everyone who had ordered them. The book had to be rather large and expensive so that a salesman could make enough money selling it to pay his expenses. Dr. Kellogg figured that if canvassers could sell his book by subscription, there would be enough profits so they could support themselves.

George, meanwhile, was busy selling small booklets and subscriptions to our magazines, including *The Health Reformer,* in a place called Belleville, Ontario, not far from Toronto. On February 1 of 1879 he wrote a letter that was published in the *Review and Herald* magazine to encourage all the members. He said, "This is a hard field, but prejudice seems to be giving way. I have obtained 125 subscriptions for our periodicals; and in subscriptions and for books sales have received $145." When I read that, about George working in a "hard field," I knew he hadn't changed. No way would George King ever work anywhere but in the hardest fields.

Later that year I read in the *Review* how George was helping another minister holding tent meetings, visiting with the people and even helping with the preaching and singing at the meetings. As the years went by, I heard many times that George had developed into a very good preacher. He could have done it full time, I'm sure; yet he felt that the special call he had received in our living room that afternoon after trying to preach was to a different kind of ministry—the fireside ministry—and was for him much more important.

In 1880, as Dr. Kellogg's 1600-page book was about to come off the presses, Dr. Kellogg began recruiting young men to sell it. He got the best there were: George King and two others, a Mr. Wilcox and a Mr. Hughes. All three came to Battle Creek, where Dr. Kellogg personally taught them everything he had learned from other publishers about selling large books by subscription.

I was still attending Battle Creek College at that time; so George and I spent some time together, talking.

He had changed a lot in seven years of hard labor, selling books in Canada. He was thirty-three years old, and I was nineteen. Though I wouldn't admit it to him, he was still a "hero" to me, just as he had been that winter on our farm, when he practiced so hard trying to become a preacher. George had grown a full beard, but I could still see a lot of lines on his face—especially around his eyes. I guess it was those many hours of walking from farm to farm with the sun beating down—or in the winter with the wind blowing the snow in his face—that caused them. I told him that he should take better care of himself, eat more regularly, and spend a little more money on clothing that would keep him warm.

But George hardly listened to anything I would say. He was very excited about this new idea of selling books by subscription, and he talked on and on about the possibilities of hundreds of colporteurs, scattered all over the country, selling by subscription, earning enough to support themselves, winning converts, and raising up churches in places where there had been no Adventists before. He was as enthusiastic now about his work as he had been about his desire to preach.

He and Mr. Wilcox and Mr. Hughes left for Indiana on July 6, 1880. I walked down to the train station to see him off. In a way, it was like all the times I had walked out to the main road with him to see him off on his first weeks of canvassing. He had a carpetbag full of material—the prospectus for the *Home Hand Book* and all additional space full of literature to give away or sell. He didn't dress any better now than he had seven years ago. And he had that same excitement, that same urgency to get out and sell books, and tell others of the message, that he had had in those earlier days. He stood on the back steps of the last car of the train, and I waved until the train had rounded a bend.

As I walked back to the college, I wondered if it would be another seven years before I would see him again.

8

I didn't have to wait another seven years to see George again. He was back in town in just less than a year and a half, excited about a new idea for his "ministry."

The subscription sales of the *Home Hand Book* written by Dr. Kellogg, and being sold door to door down in Indiana by Mr. Wilcox and Mr. Hughes and himself, had gone well. So well, in fact, that he had realized that here, in selling by subscription, was the answer to the dream that had possessed him all these years. Here was a way for canvassers to sell religious books full time and make a living doing it—a way to get hundreds of men and women into this type of ministry, going door to door, across the country. He could hardly wait to tell of his dream.

But he had a problem. He didn't have a book to sell. At that time the Review and Herald printed no religious books anywhere near the size or the price of Dr. Kellogg's *Home Hand Book.* The only books of any size were Mrs. White's *The Spirit of Prophecy,* three volumes that were later expanded into what is now the Conflict of the Ages series, and two books by Uriah Smith, *Thoughts on Daniel* and *Thoughts on the Revelation.* None of these was large enough or illustrated in such a way as to be used by subscription book salesmen.

George felt that religious books could be sold by subscription, and he proposed to prove it with a trial edition combining *Thoughts on Daniel* and *Thoughts on the Revelation* into one volume. Together the two books would be large enough to sell by subscription; and George felt that with some good illustrations they would be an outstanding success.

So he returned to Battle Creek in December of 1881, during the time of the General Conference session, and proceeded to convince the brethren to give the project a try. He had with him his own two copies of *Daniel* and *Revelation*—the same ones my father, Richard Godsmark, had given him years before. He would put the two books together to show their combined size and tell how he had been successful selling *Home Hand Book* by subscription and how he could do it with *Daniel* and *Revelation* if they would just print the two books in one.

The management of the Review and Herald was very reluctant to try this new idea. All the religious books they had printed up to this time had been designed for sale only to Adventist believers—no one had ever sold books in any quantity to non-Adventists. If the idea failed, the Review could lose a lot of money, because it took the typesetting department many hours of time to set a book into type, particularly a book as large as the one George King was proposing. Once they set a book into type, they could print one copy or a hundred thousand copies; the major work was done. They figured that they would have to sell at least a thousand copies to break even.

"Brethren," he would say, waving his copies of *Daniel* and *Revelation,* pressed tightly together, "print a trial edition of 5000 copies, and I will personally guarantee to sell 1000 myself."

When some of the ministers and the management of the Review looked skeptical, George would quote from Ellen White's testimony how we should obey her counsel to sell the books from house to house.

"We've got to have a book with good

illustrations," George would say. "Get Uriah Smith to engrave some wooden plates with pictures of great Babylon and hard-riding Turks and the horrible beasts of prophecy. Print them in black and red, and that book will sell."

"Give it some handsome bindings—let the customer choose between leather and cloth. Price it high enough so that canvassers can make money, enough to stay in the field, selling more books and see what happens," George would say.

In the end, George must have talked to every minister there in Battle Creek for the session, because it paid off. The Review decided to accept his challenge and print the books.

And it did just as he had suggested. Uriah Smith himself, the very man who had written the books, and who had, in earlier years, been a wood engraver, engraved the picture of the great and horrible beast of Daniel 7 to be in two colors, showing the blood around its claws and its mouth.

Some books would have a cloth binding, blue and green fine-twined linen. Some would have a sheepskin binding, and others, morocco with marbled or gilt edges.

The Review and Herald promised George

that the books would be ready during the first part of April 1882; so George went to work getting orders.

By January 10, only a couple of weeks after the Review promised to print the books, George had his first orders.

He went to Ohio, where he trained a group of twelve canvassers who would sell the book there.

Then, as the time drew closer when the Review said it would have the first books, George got a job working at the Lewis broom factory in Battle Creek, sorting broomcorn, so he would be on hand as the books came off the press. Working alongside him was a young man by the name of Webb Reavis; and as the hours and days passed by, all George could talk about was the possibilities of selling *Daniel and the Revelation* by subscription and using religious book sales to spread the truth.

On April 3, 1882, the very day the first books were due to come off the press, George King arrived at the factory where he worked by nine o'clock in the morning. The Review was as true to its word as George was to his, it delivered to him the first copy that morning. George took it back to the broom factory and went from worker to worker, showing the new

book that he planned to sell by subscription and that would change the way the colporteurs worked. When George got to Webb Reavis, he insisted that Webb buy the first book, for "good luck." Webb laughed at the idea.

"George," he said. "why should I buy this book, when I already have everything on Daniel and Revelation in the two separate volumes I have at home?"

But George persisted, and finally Webb gave up arguing and paid $2.50 for the first copy of the book ever to come off the presses.

Just as George had planned, the book was expensive. With the blue and green linen binding, it cost $1.50. With sheepskin binding, it was $2.50. With morocco, $4.00, and with marbled or gilt edges, $5.00.

And it sold, just as George had predicted that it would. By July, 1500 copies of the new edition had been sold. By November, George and others had organized canvassers working as far away as the Dakota Territory.

But even George King had little idea how far his concept of selling books by subscription would go. *Daniel and the Revelation* was one of the all-time great-selling books. Several years later *The Great Controversy* was published, followed by *Bible Readings for the Home Circle,* and many others. Within ten years 500 full-time colporteurs were at work in the United States with another 100 in other countries. They sold so many books that the production of the Review and Herald was almost tripled.

I graduated from college about this time and went into the ministry in the Michigan and Indiana Conferences. I married Cora Shepherd in 1886, and shortly thereafter moved to Los Angeles, California, to begin the work on the West Coast.

George King, meanwhile, seemed to be all over the country, selling books wherever there was a particularly hard territory to work in, and training others for the literature ministry. He worked in Colorado and New Mexico. Then he was down south, working in various Southern States. He took a trip to British Guiana, in South America, and sold $900 worth of books before the climate made him ill and forced him to return to the United States. Later, he took another trip to Jamaica, where he sold several thousand dollars' worth of books. After his trip to Jamaica, he decided that New York City was the most difficult field in the world to work in; so that was the place for him, and he spent the next nineteen years working in the streets of that great city.

I heard from him only occasionally as the years went by. Sometimes I would read an article by George in the *Review,* or a short note telling of the progress of the work—especially the literature ministry—in New York City. Or I would hear about him from someone who had known him or seen him recently.

I remember one story I heard about him that made me laugh—it sounded so much like the determined, dedicated George King I had known as a boy. It seems that the brethren in Washington, D.C., where the General Conference headquarters had been moved after the fires in Battle Creek, invited George, who was in New York, to come and speak on the colporteur work at the Annual Council to be held in Battle Creek. George wrote back: "What do I have to say that would be of any special help? Besides," he said, "if I came down, I would have to sit in the cars [railroad cars] a night and a day, and then sit in a conference a week, and in the cars again to get back home, which is something to be dreaded." George felt he could spend the time far better selling books in New York City.

George was always very modest about his own achievements, but I heard it said that he admitted once that he must have sold over

$25,000 worth of books and other literature. I'm sure, if all the facts were known, that in his lifetime he sold far more than that.

George died in New York City in 1906 at fifty-nine years of age. After quite a few years in the ministry, I studied medicine, and became a doctor in Chattanooga, Tennessee. I always felt that the reason George died so young was all those years he spent working through heat and cold, summer and winter, always on his feet, traveling from place to place to tell others of the truth, to sell his beloved books and tracts, and to teach other men and women to canvass. But then, when you think about it, the most important work that George accomplished was not all those thousands of dollars worth of books that he sold, or even all the souls that he won. His greatest work was his steadfast devotion to the literature ministry, and his ideas for selling religious books by subscription, that founded the entire colporteur work.

George is resting now, but in his place every day thousands of men and women and boys and girls go out, selling millions of dollars' worth of books and magazines containing the truth—and they will be doing it until the Lord comes.